ANIMAL SECRETS

BY RANDALL HARTSELL

ISBN 978-1-70517-291-9

WILLIS MUSIC

Exclusively Distributed By

Hal•Leonard®

Visit Hal Leonard Online at
www.halleonard.com

World headquarters, contact:
Hal Leonard
7777 West Bluemound Road
Milwaukee, WI 53213
Email: info@halleonard.com

In Europe, contact:
Hal Leonard Europe Limited
42 Wigmore Street
Marylebone, London, W1U 2RN
Email: info@halleonardeurope.com

In Australia, contact:
Hal Leonard Australia Pty. Ltd.
4 Lentara Court
Cheltenham, Victoria, 3192 Australia
Email: info@halleonard.com.au

FROM THE COMPOSER

If you sit quietly with our animal friends, they often reveal secrets about their lives. Animals are amazing creatures and share many traits with humans.

You may have secrets and treasures inside of you that you would love to share with friends. Sometimes we should talk less and listen more so we can better understand who our friends are inside.

Below I share some people traits that each animal brought to my mind. After playing a piece (make sure to play *and* sing!), share with your teacher and family other traits you see in each creature.

I invite you to take time whenever you can to sit alone and observe our special creatures and protect them and their habitat from harm.

Rendell Wartelle

ANIMAL TRAITS AND SECRETS

Caterpillar Crawl	Being a late bloomer is okay.
Cool as a Puffin	Sometimes you have to play peacemaker.
Crows Have All Their Marbles	Still waters can run deep. Intelligence is important.
The Difference Between My Cat and a Lion	It's okay to be different. Some are brave and loving, others lazy and loving!
Dolphin Love	Treasure loyalty, and appreciate friends who are cheerful and playful, and who lift you up when you are sad.
One Smart Octopus	The ability to be resourceful and think quickly on your feet is essential.
Pigs with Pearls	Have pride in yourself (and especially your fashion sense)!
Porcupine Pal	We should always support our friends, especially during hard times.
Shark!	Overcoming fear and doubt can bring strength and protectiveness.
Squirrel Problems	We should all have a sense of humor and be able to laugh at ourselves!

CONTENTS

One Smart Octopus

Words and Music by
Randall Hartsell

Lively

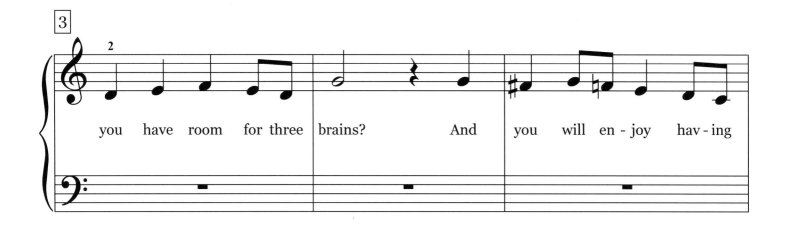

Are you as smart as an oc - to - pus? Do

you have room for three brains? And you will en - joy hav - ing

six more arms to play Bach when you en - ter -

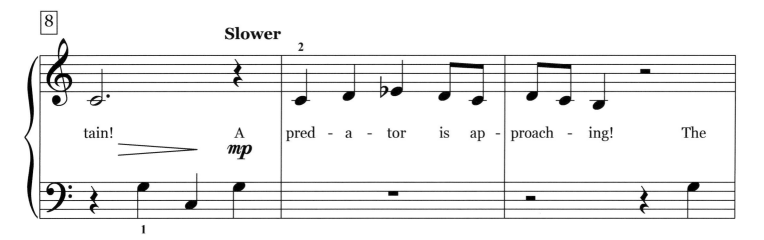

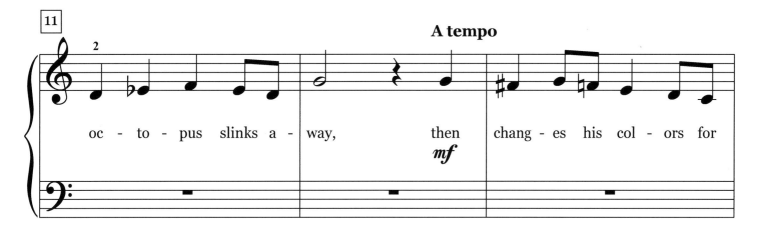

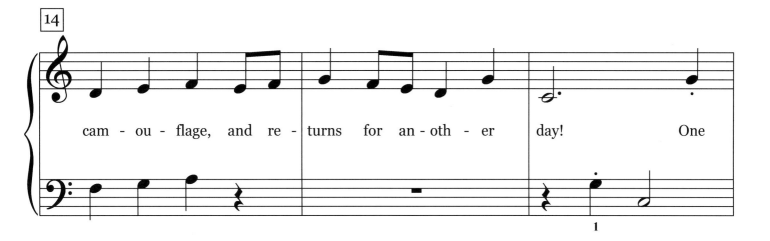

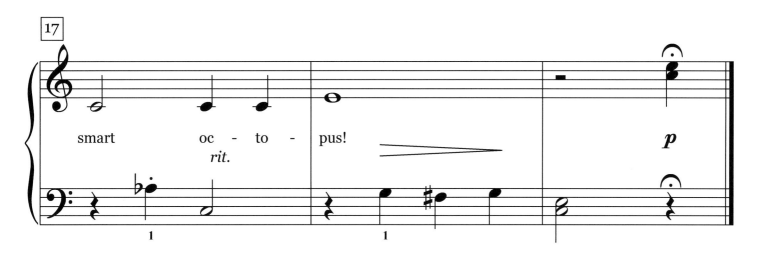

5

Porcupine Pal

Words and Music by
Randall Hartsell

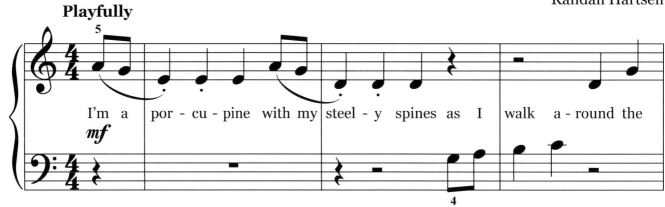

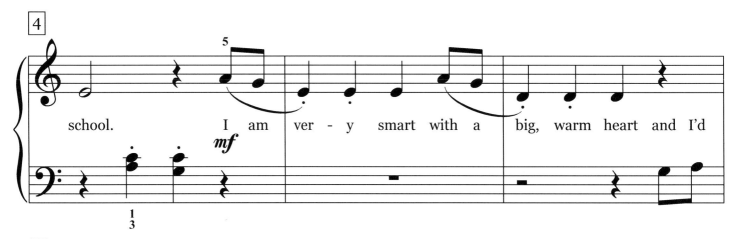

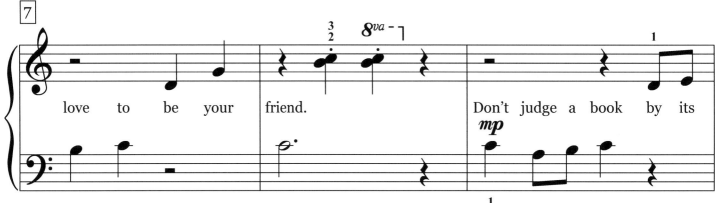

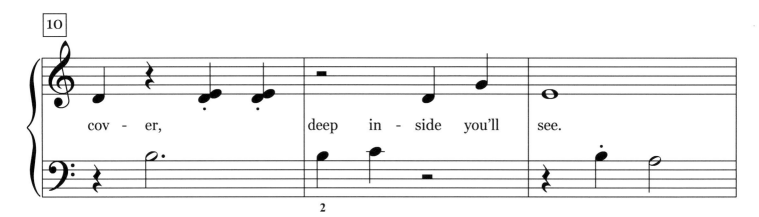

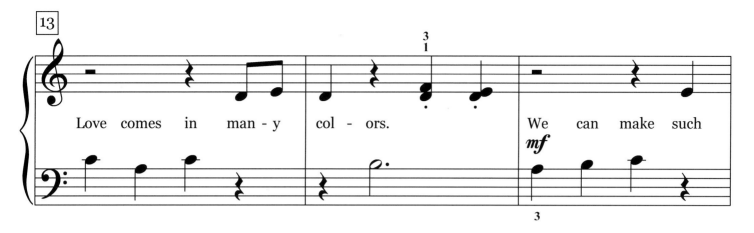

13

Love comes in man - y col - ors. We can make such

16

har - mon - y. If a por - cu - pine should ask you to dine with her

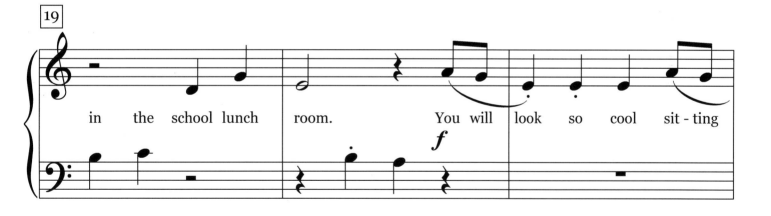

19

in the school lunch room. You will look so cool sit - ting

22

on your stool with the best friend in the world.

Dolphin Love

Words and Music by
Randall Hartsell

Moderately

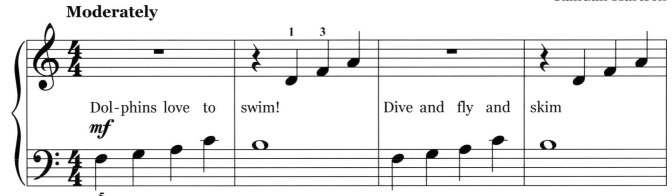

Pedal only when you think the dolphins are under water.

Dol-phins love to swim! Dive and fly and skim

through deep wa - ters, through the seas, all while wink - ing "hi" at me!

Dol-phins love to swim, grey and sleek and trim. Swirl-ing, twirl-ing

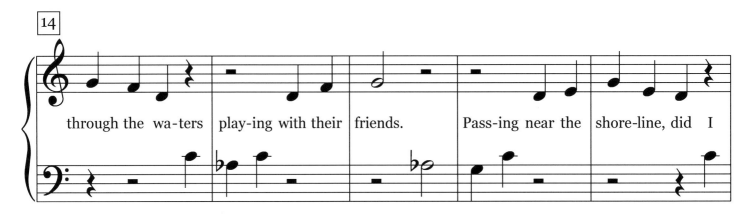

through the wa-ters play-ing with their friends. Pass-ing near the shore-line, did I

19 see a joy-ful grin? O-ver, un-der man-y waves, ev-'ry one is

24 blithe and brave. Swim-ming out and back a-gain with ease.

29 Dol-phins love to swim! Dive and fly and skim

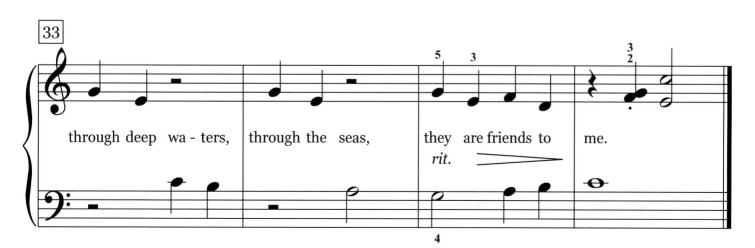

33 through deep wa-ters, through the seas, they are friends to me.

Caterpillar Crawl

Words and Music by
Randall Hartsell

Cheerfully, at a moderate pace

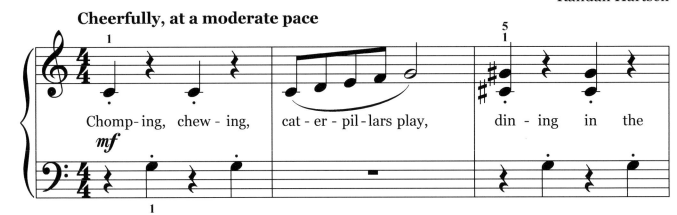

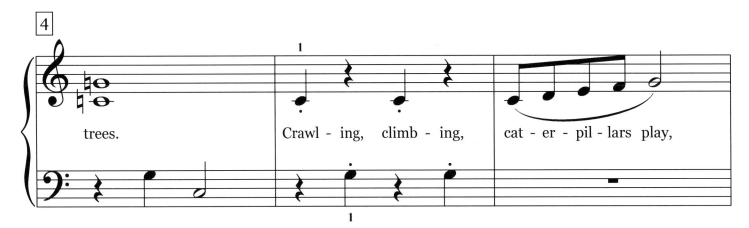

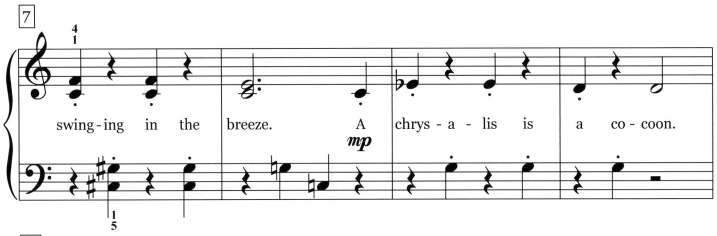

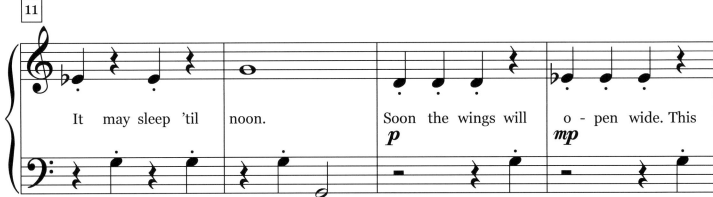

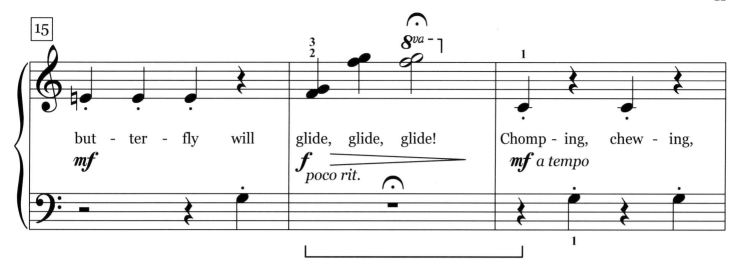

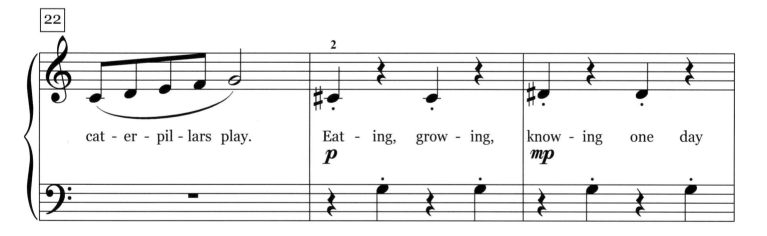

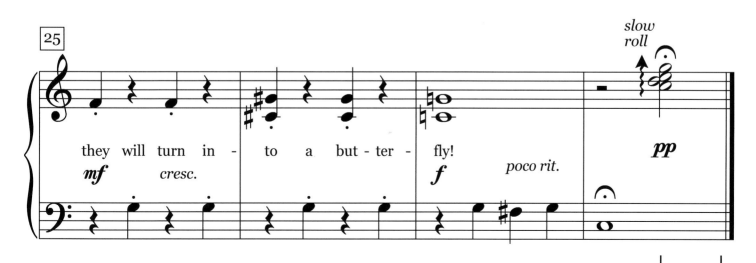

Cool as a Puffin

Words and Music by
Randall Hartsell

With a swagger

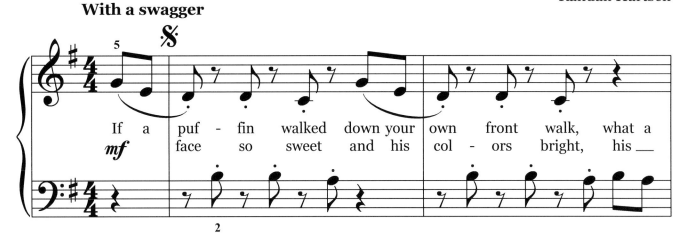

If a puf - fin walked down your own front walk, what a
face so sweet and his col - ors bright, his ___

sight this bird would be. With his or - ange feet and his
smile would make *you* smile. And with man - ners kind and a

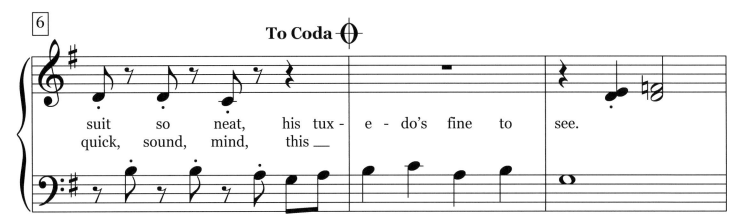

To Coda

suit so neat, his tux - e - do's fine to see.
quick, sound, mind, this ___

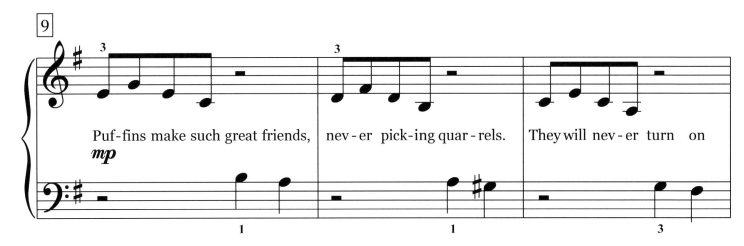

Puf-fins make such great friends, nev - er pick-ing quar - rels. They will nev - er turn on

you.

Nev-er seek-ing con-flict,

peace is what they work for.

mf

Fly-ing in the winds,

mak-ing sure his neigh-bor's hap-py. —

poco rit.

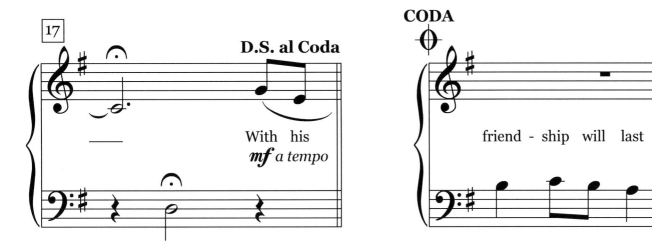

D.S. al Coda

With his

mf *a tempo*

CODA

friend-ship will last a -

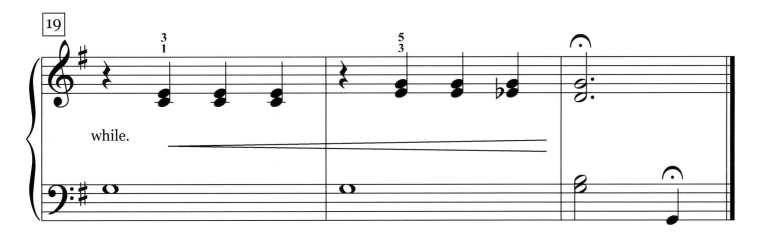

while.

Pigs with Pearls

Words and Music by
Randall Hartsell

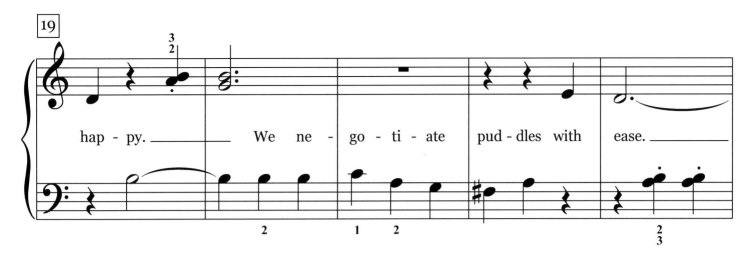

hap - py. ____ We ne - go - ti - ate pud - dles with ease. ____

____ Please do not sneer when you see me walk by. ____

D.S. al Coda

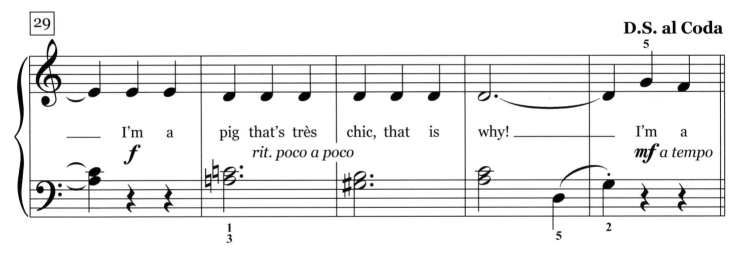

____ I'm a pig that's très chic, that is why! ____ I'm a

f   *rit. poco a poco*   *mf a tempo*

CODA

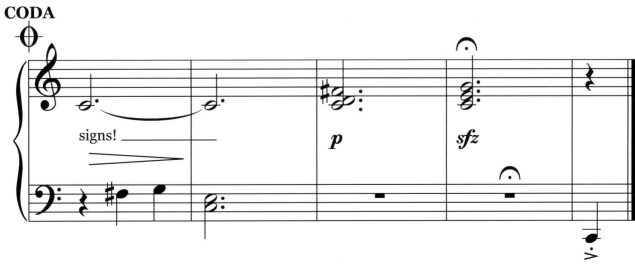

signs! ____

p   *sfz*

Squirrel Problems

Words and Music by
Randall Hartsell

Moderately, with a lilt

*Wiggle ever so slightly

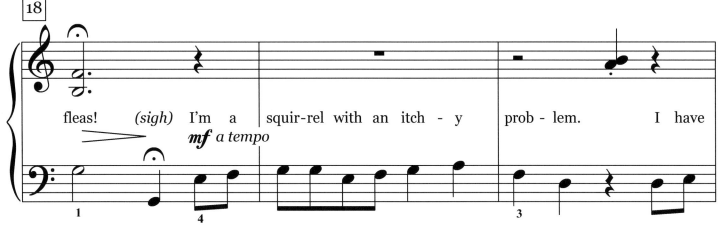

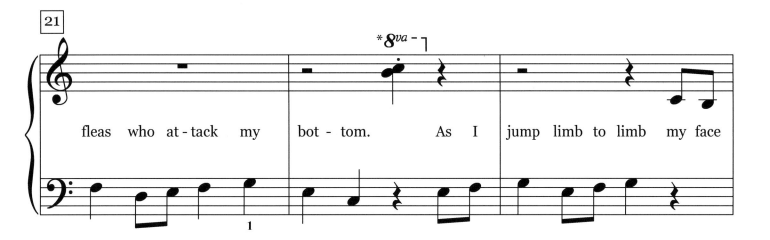

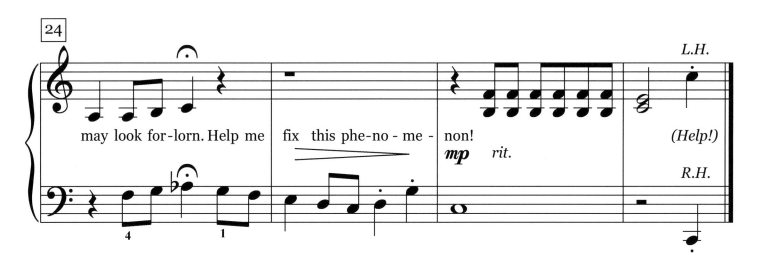

Crows Have All Their Marbles

Words and Music by
Randall Hartsell

sits near a cloud. She loves to ride on a breeze. _____ The

com-mon crow is not com-mon at all. They're one big fam-i - ly. They

strut and squawk, e - ven read traf-fic lights! Their prais - es should be

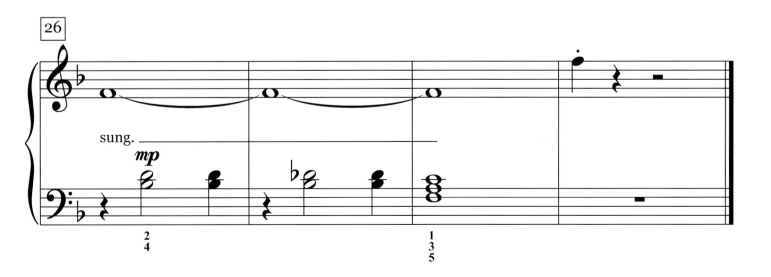

sung. _____

The Difference Between
My Cat and a Lion

Words and Music by
Randall Hartsell

* *There are no wrong notes in cluster chords! Right hand crosses over the left hand into the bowels of the piano. Use your whole palm to create a deep roar.*

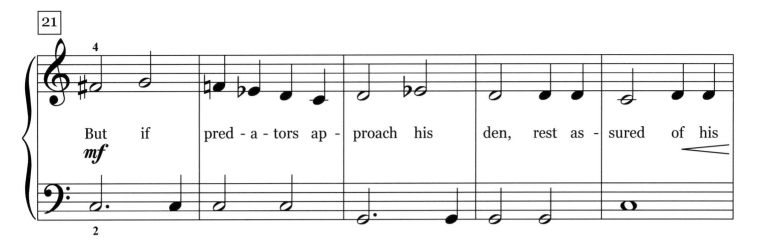

But if pred - a - tors ap - proach his den, rest as - sured of his

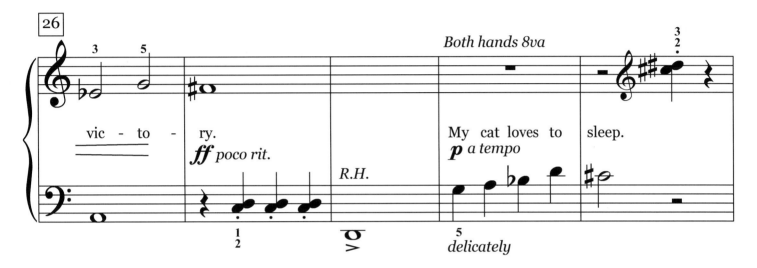

vic - to - ry. My cat loves to sleep.

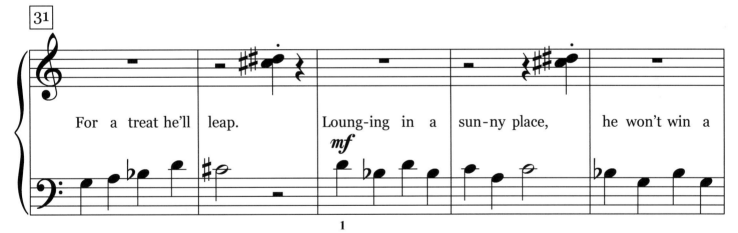

For a treat he'll leap. Loung-ing in a sun-ny place, he won't win a

kit - ty race. My cat loves to sleep. May-be he counts sheep.

Shark!

Words and Music by
Randall Hartsell

Lively, with fright

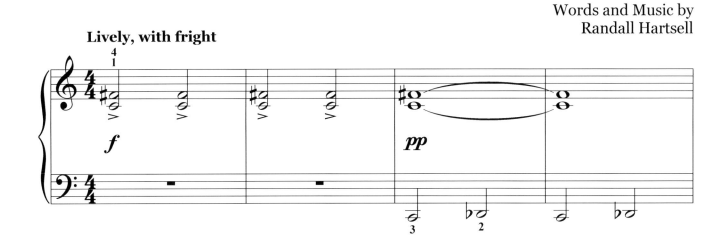

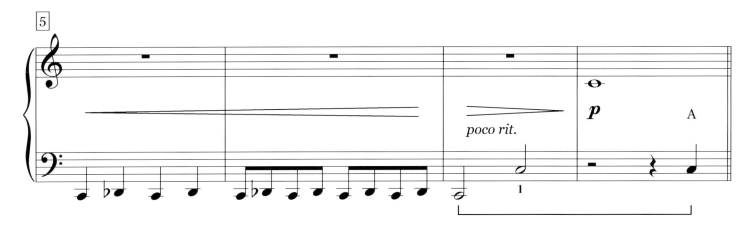

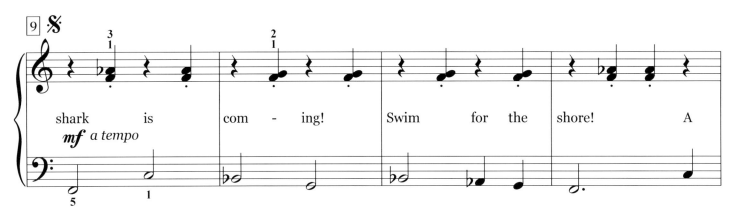

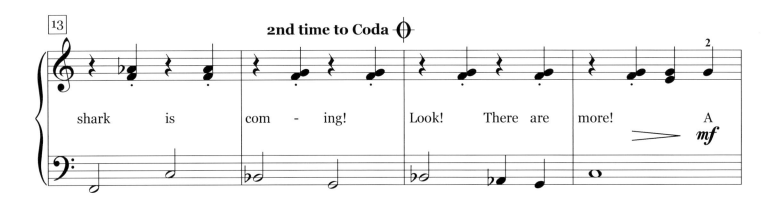

MORE

PIANO COLLECTIONS FROM WILLIS MUSIC

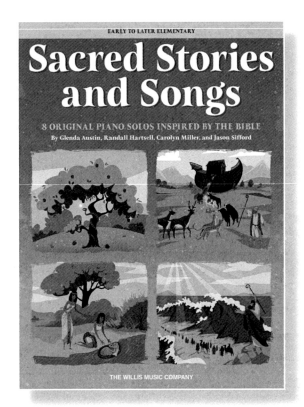